“This is Kimberly Heil’s best book to date! May you explore a visual healing as you take in the energy of the art within this book.”

–Krista Polinsky, Energy Medicine and Feng Shui Practitioner

“Visual Alchemy is a powerful book that is needed in the world today. Kimberly’s art transmutes your being as you look at the images and read the words. I especially love her commitment to the betwixt in-between places where we need time to integrate the image into our being. For me, the topics of grief and initiation compel you to want to go deeper into yourself. I love her work and this latest heartfelt creation of questing into our hearts, psyches, and souls.”

–Sarina Harz, LMSW

“Your art work and words touched my soul with a deep recognition. I so feel this book has an ability to bring excitement and rekindle a passion for the earthly gifts offered to us that we may have forgotten.”

–Jotree, Crone, Drum Maker, and Artist

Visual Alchemy

An intuitive journey through art and words

By Kimberly Heil

Written and Illustrated by Kimberly Heil
Designed by Jacquelyn Tierney

For the soul searchers, visionaries, artists, healers,
and truth seekers

Contents

Visual Alchemy

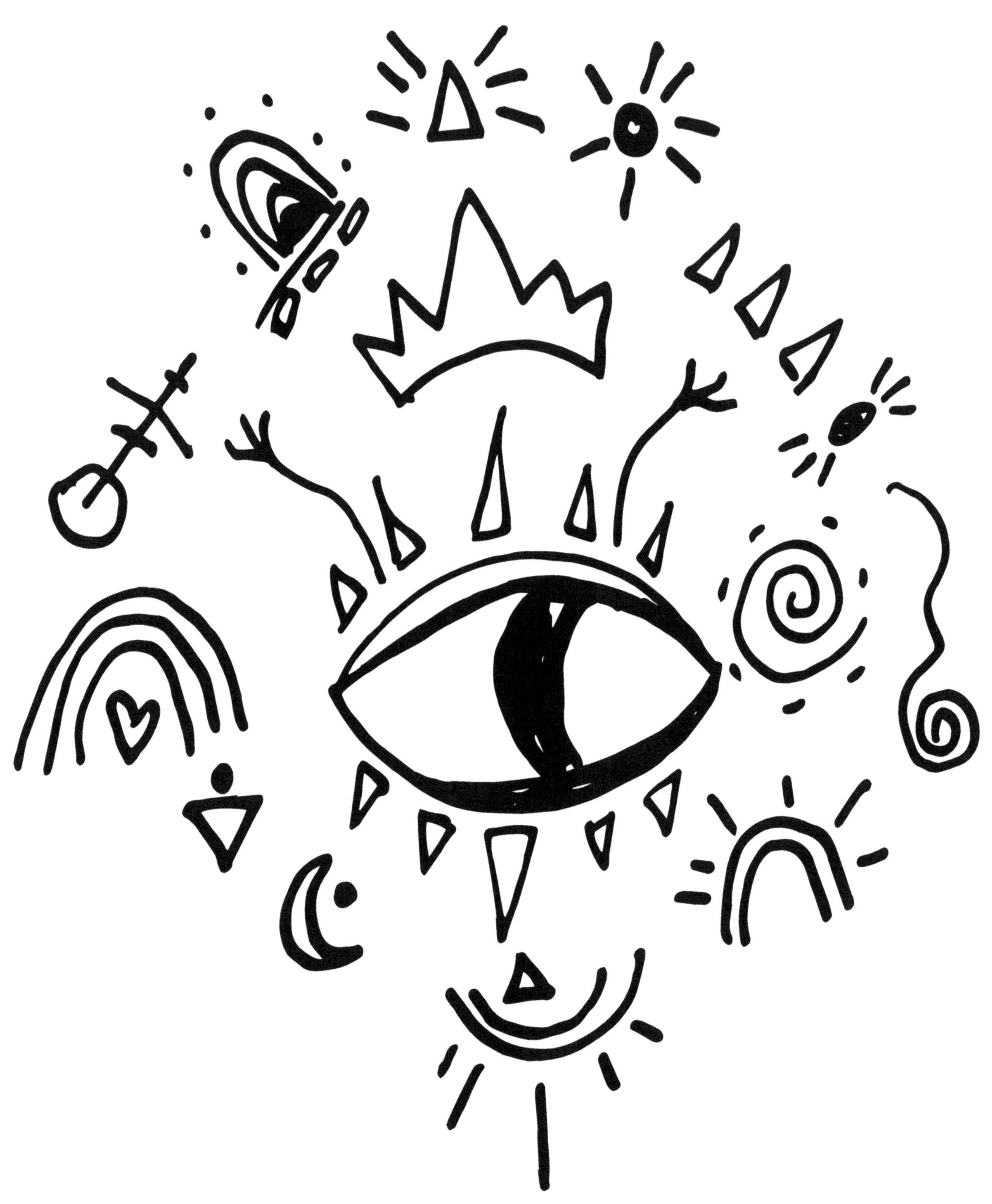

Introduction

I am a creative being
Filled with adornments of playful colors and big brushes

Amidst the backdrop of ancient cities
I return to myself several times as I create
Walking an internal labyrinth
Going within and out to mine the facets of my being

My soul's purpose is to heal with art and words
To explore the spaces
Between the layers
Between the sounds
Between the breaths

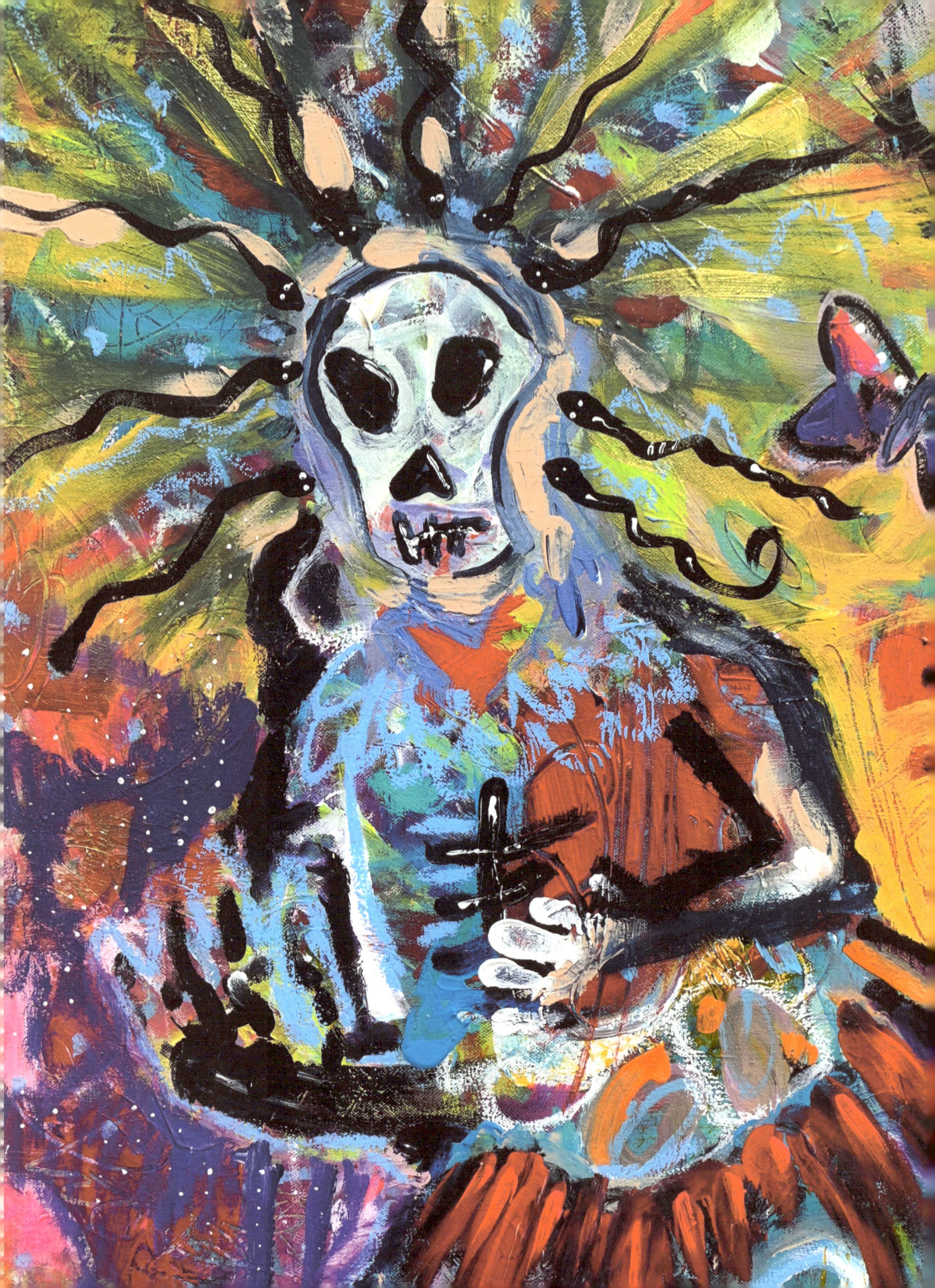

The Bone Woman

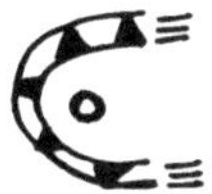

When the bone woman comes
It is time to make great shifts
Through the layers of the aura
Physically
Emotionally
Spiritually

To let go of the baggage
To lay your truths out
To engage in the world unlike any time before

One by one
Two by two
Unearthing
Excavating
The joys and the sorrows
The happiness and the tears
Shaking away the dust, the mundane, the uninspired

Laying these truths down in fire and flames
Transmuting these old ideas
Into possibility, creativity, and inspiration

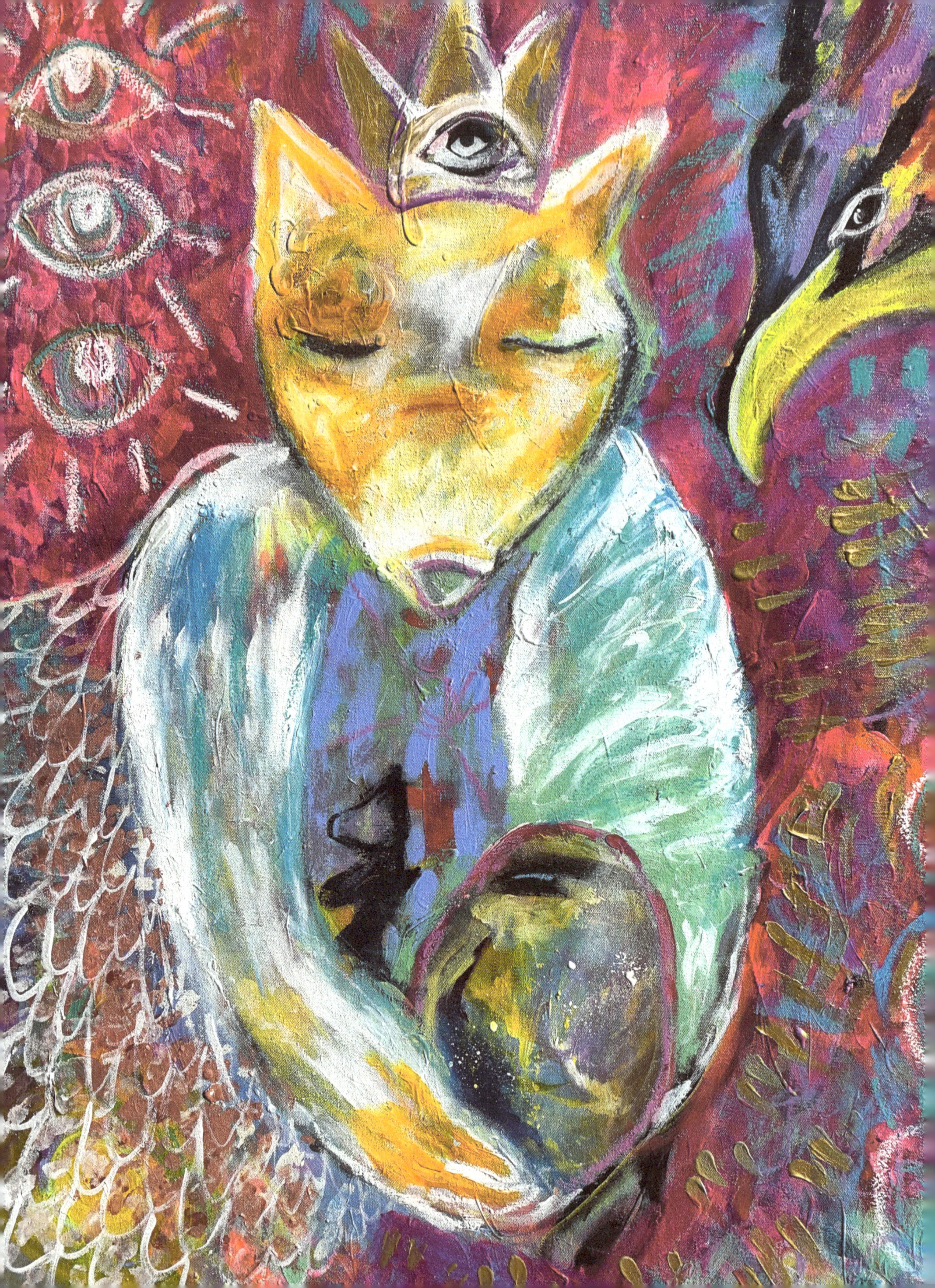

Creation

Stars collide

Worlds are born

Through cosmic winds

Swirls of stardust

Micro and macro

Begin to take form

Of lands and seas

Of animals, and humans

Combinations of Cells

In perfect forms

Give birth to a new world

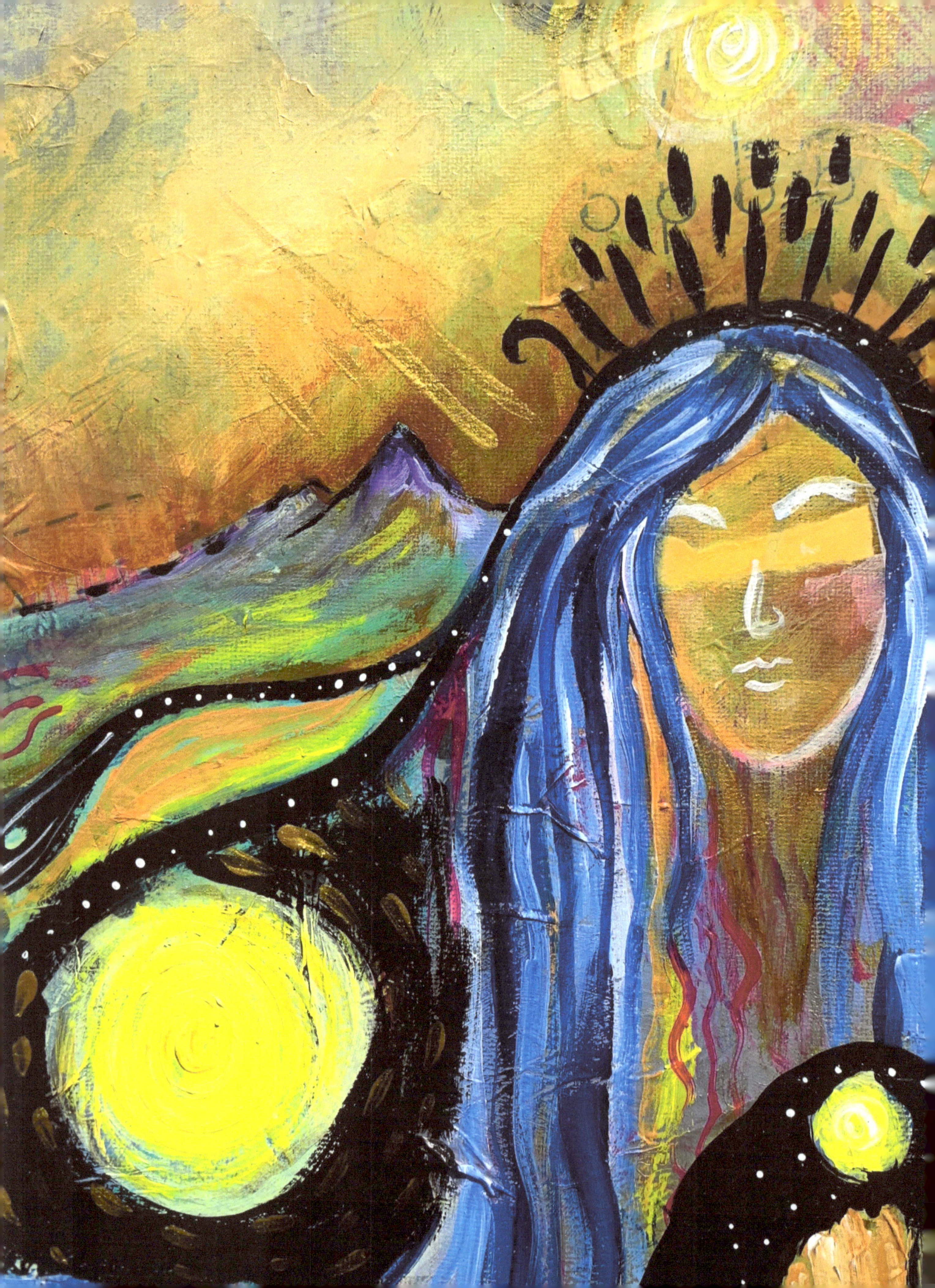

Journey

She wanted to be seen

Through the realms

Over vast landscapes

Of time

And space

She brings the stories of her ancestors

Past

Present

Future

Her vision becomes the healing

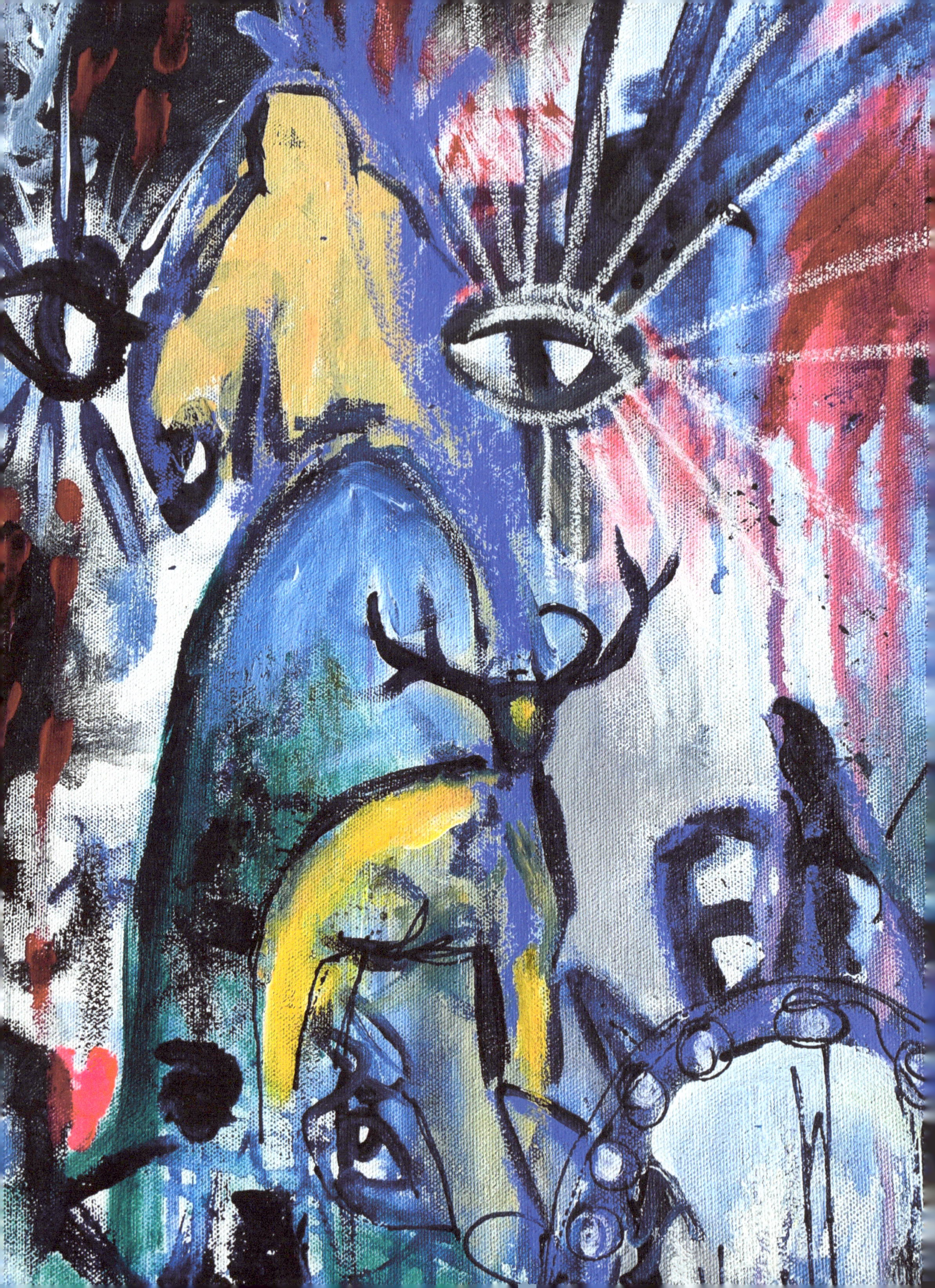

Initiation

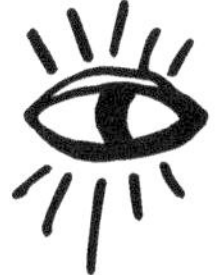

Eyes illuminate

Over the bridge of liminal space

Symbols unveiled against the universe

Visions of past, present, future

The time for reflection is here

As the Bone Woman asks...

What

 Have

  You

   Learned?

Personal stories collide with the collective unconscious

In curiosity and expanded states

Sacred truths awakened

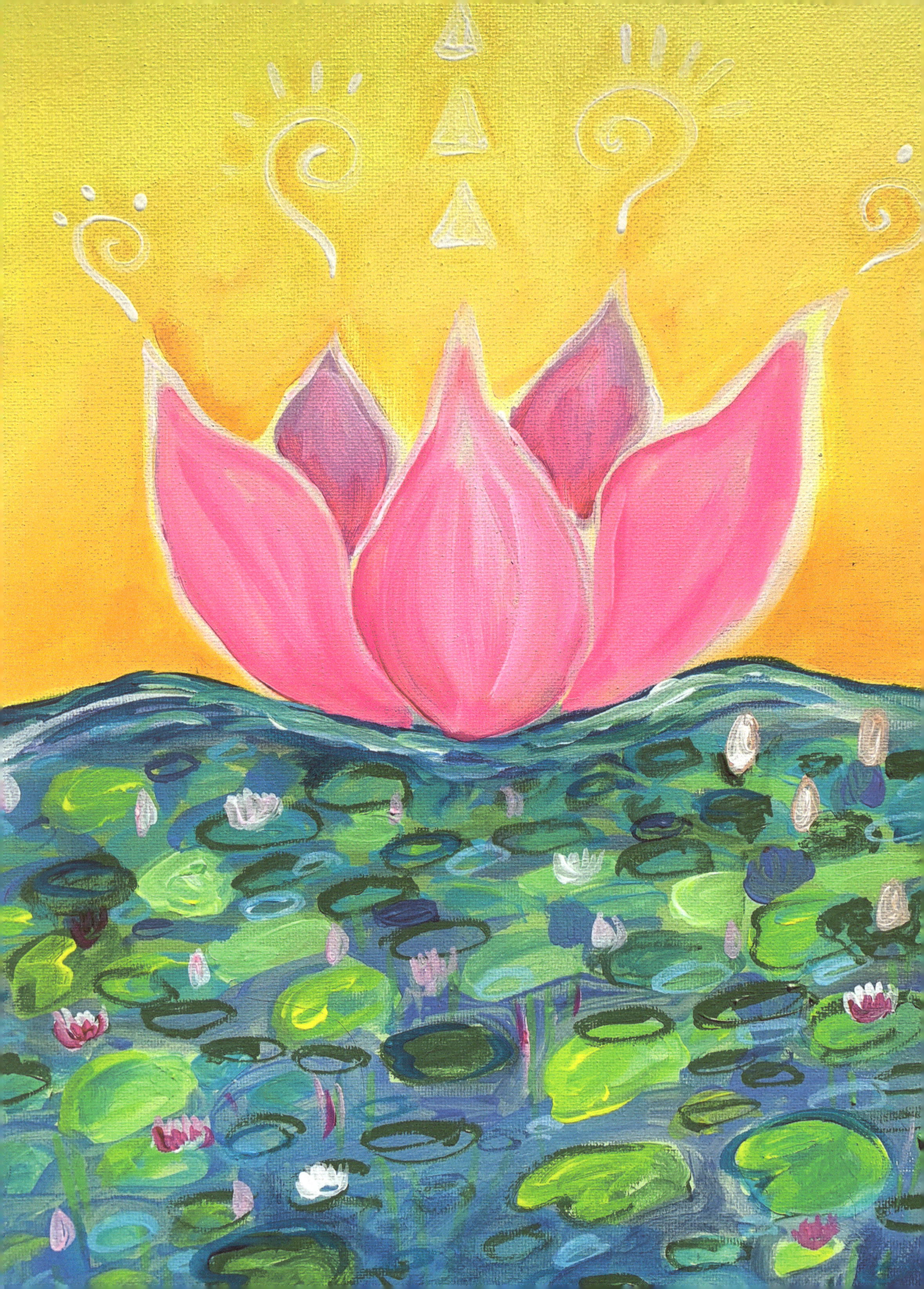

Transformation

Try

Fail

Try again

Try something different

New

Crazy

Absurd

Try

Fail

Try

Success

Out of the failures

Out of the successes

Out of determination

A lotus blooms

With a message ... Keep going

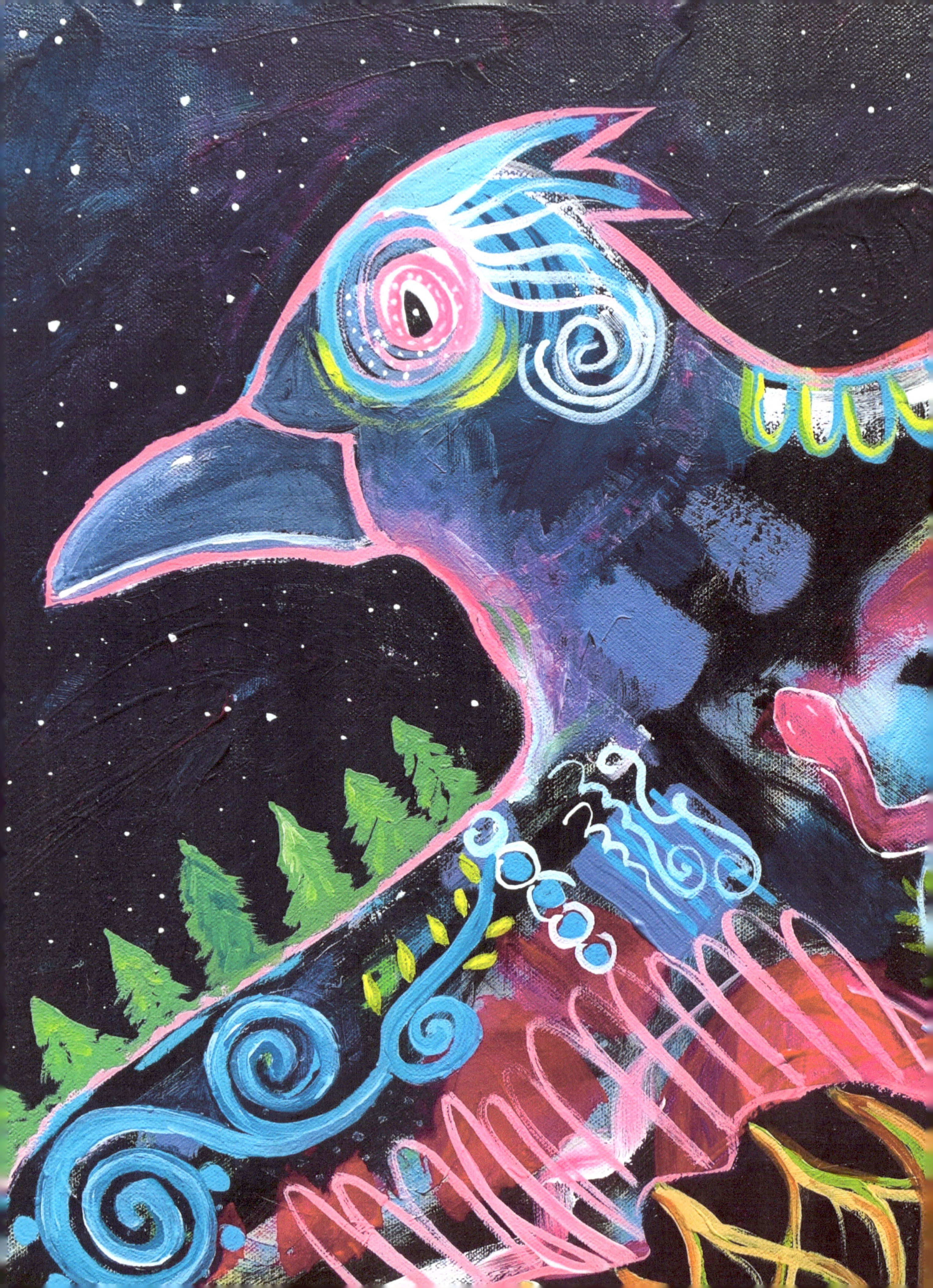

Rhythms

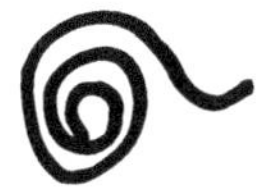

As the night comes

Crow takes flight

Witnessing the changes beneath her

The flow of the rivers

The terrain of the mountains

The call of the wolves

She watches nature in harmony with itself

Gentle rhythms and interactions that have been around for centuries

A balance of give and take

Of death and rebirth

Of transformation and desire

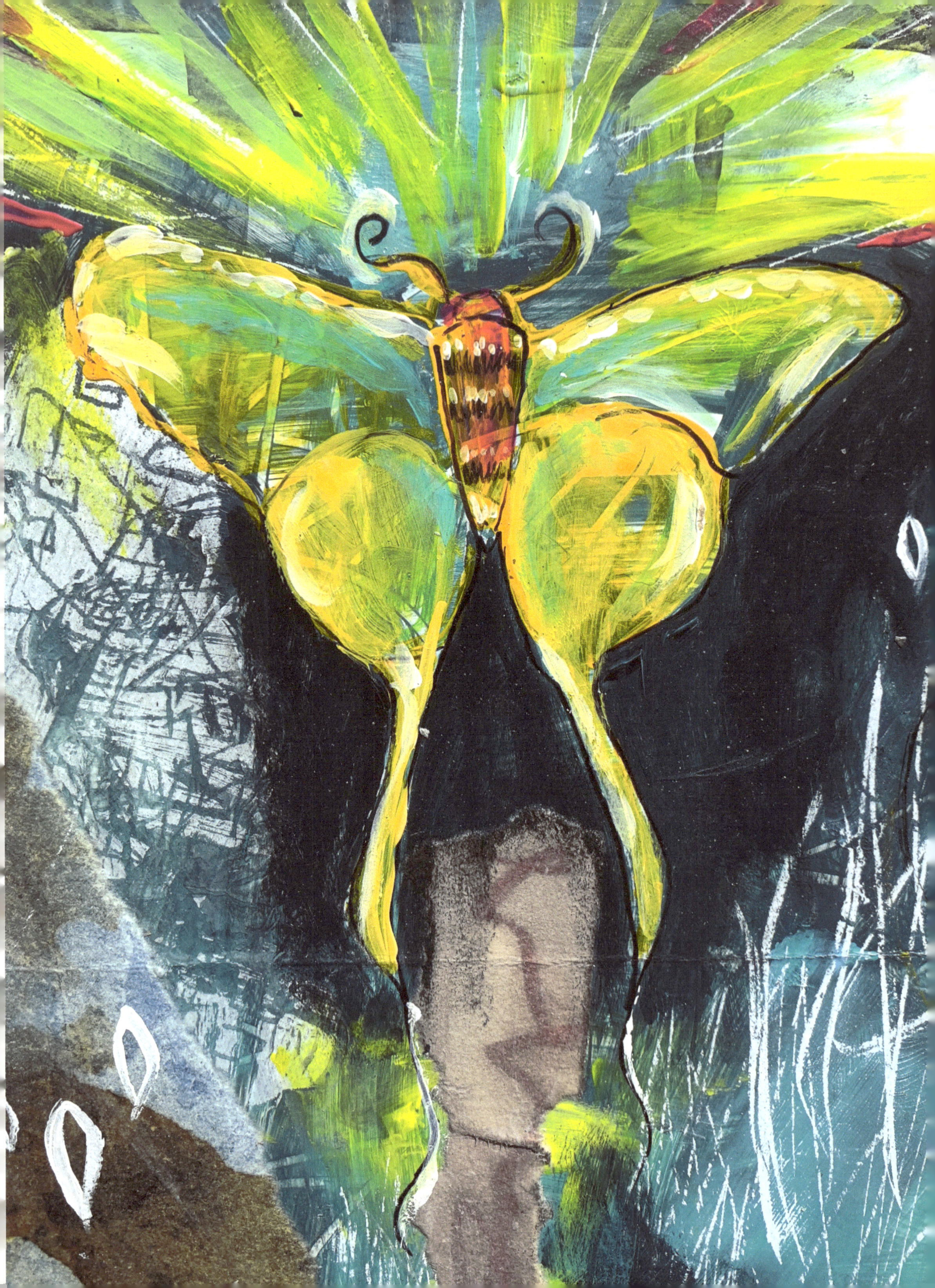

Becoming

Emerging into the world

Embodied light

Wings spread wide

A joy

A freedom

A release

Embracing a new iteration of being

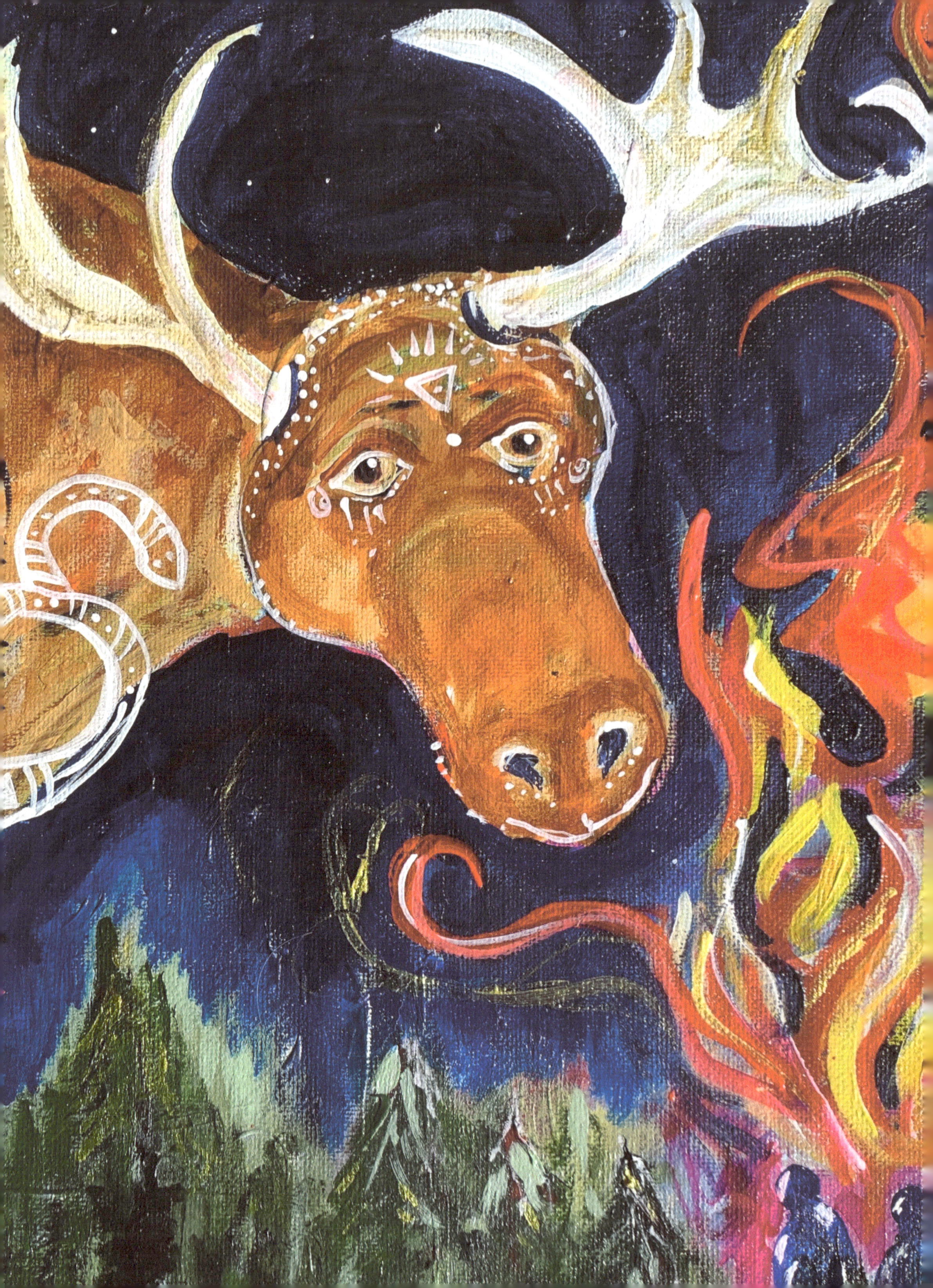

Council

By the full moonlit skies
A council of elders gathers
Among the ancient trees
Speaking their stories
Of beginnings and endings
Of time and travel
Of connection and dissonance
Animals come to hear the tales
Taking the wisdom into bone and marrow
Lineage transcribed into their DNA

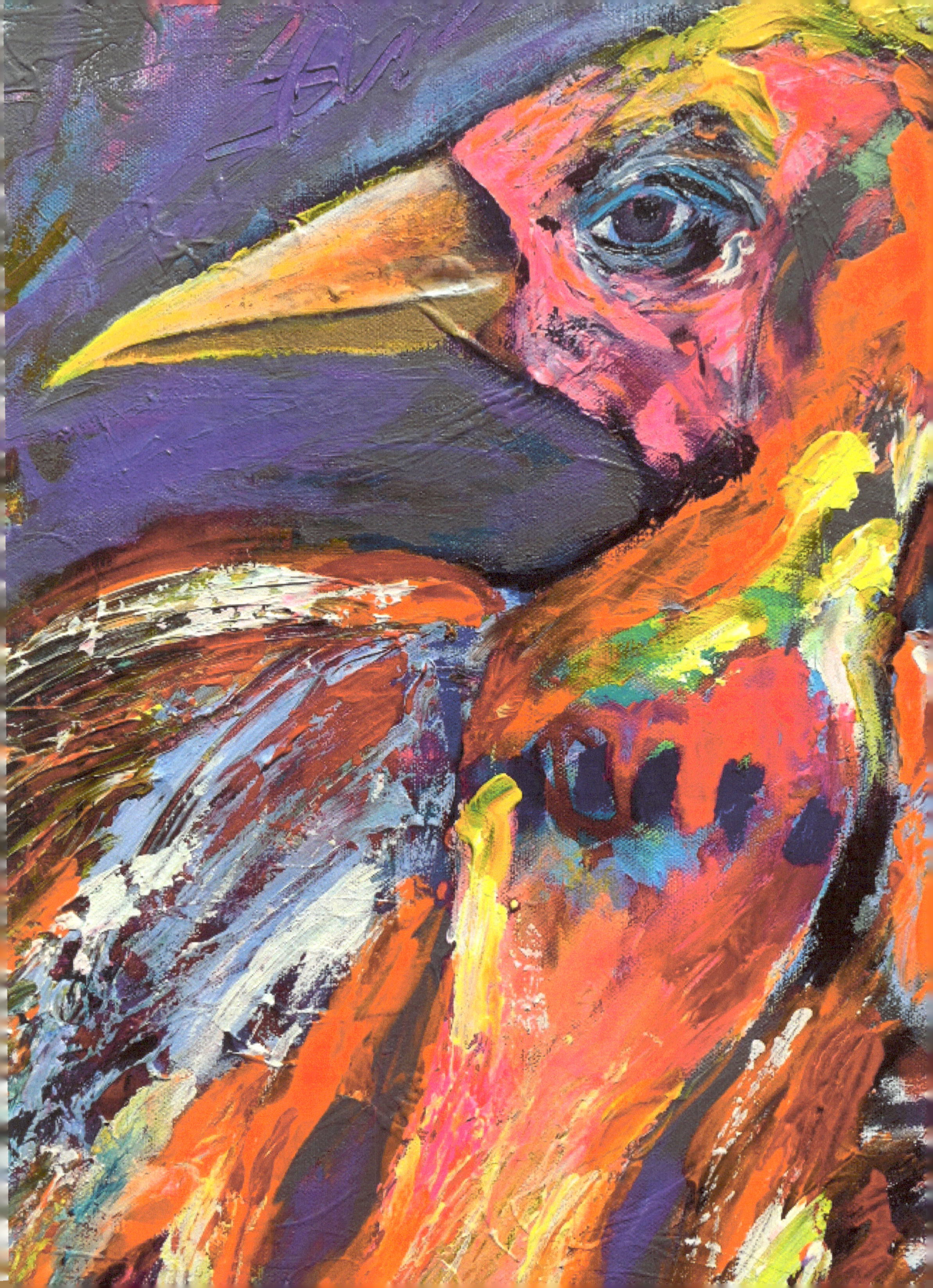

Phoenix

Dancing heat of

Fire and flames

This Dismantled archetype

Transcends dimensions

Awakening...

Stronger

Wiser

Sharper

Clear

Skillfully re-birthed

To recreate a new life

Phoenix rises

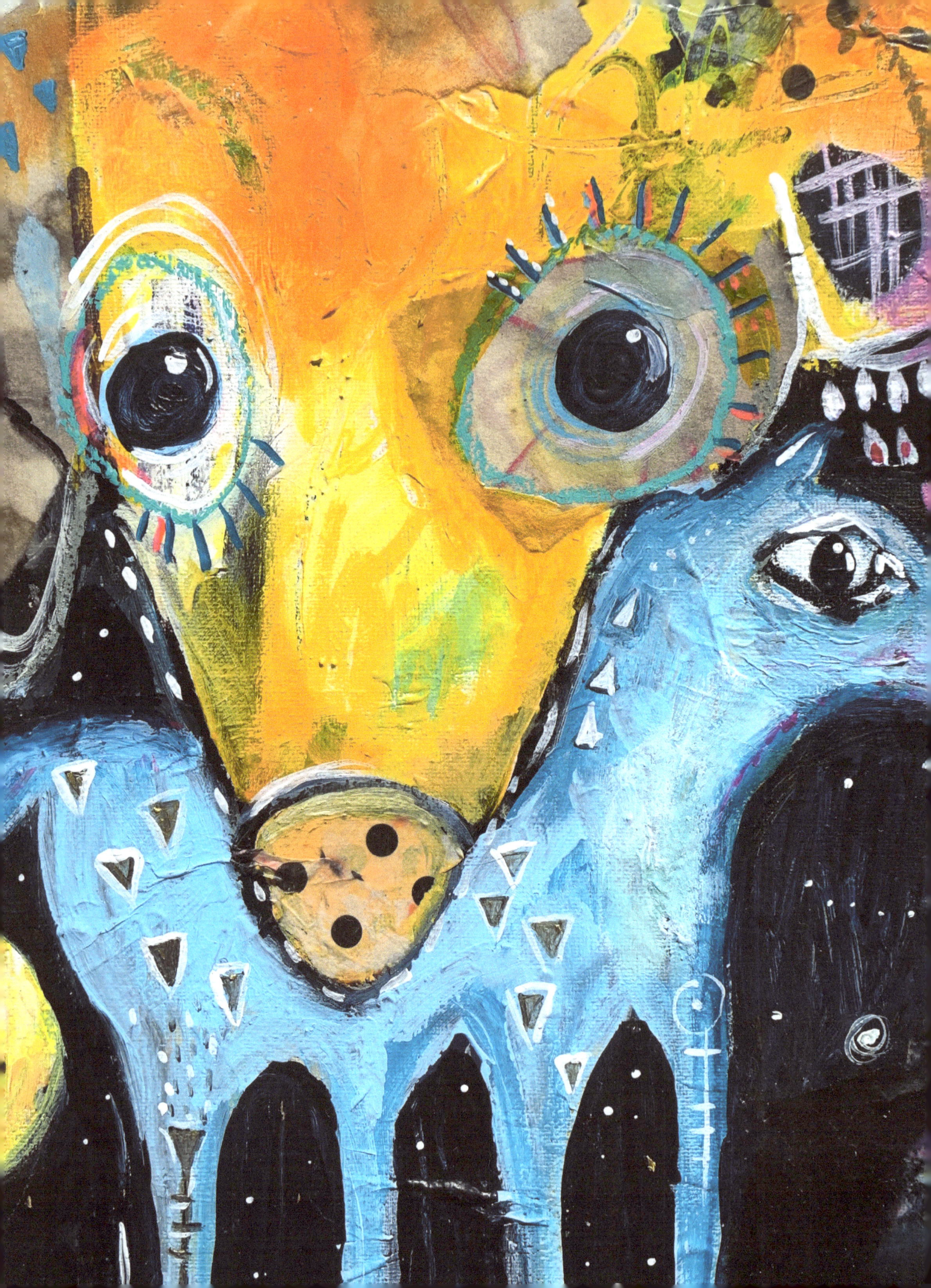

Grief

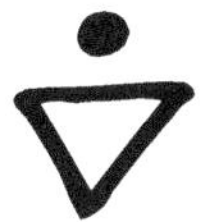

You are gone

No longer in physical form

The lessons you shared

Shine like stars in a night sky

That are held within my heart

A way of navigation when I am unsure

Always cheering me on,

Telling me 'you got this'

In art and in love

In paint and in living

You will be with me through time and space

Through lifetimes and back again

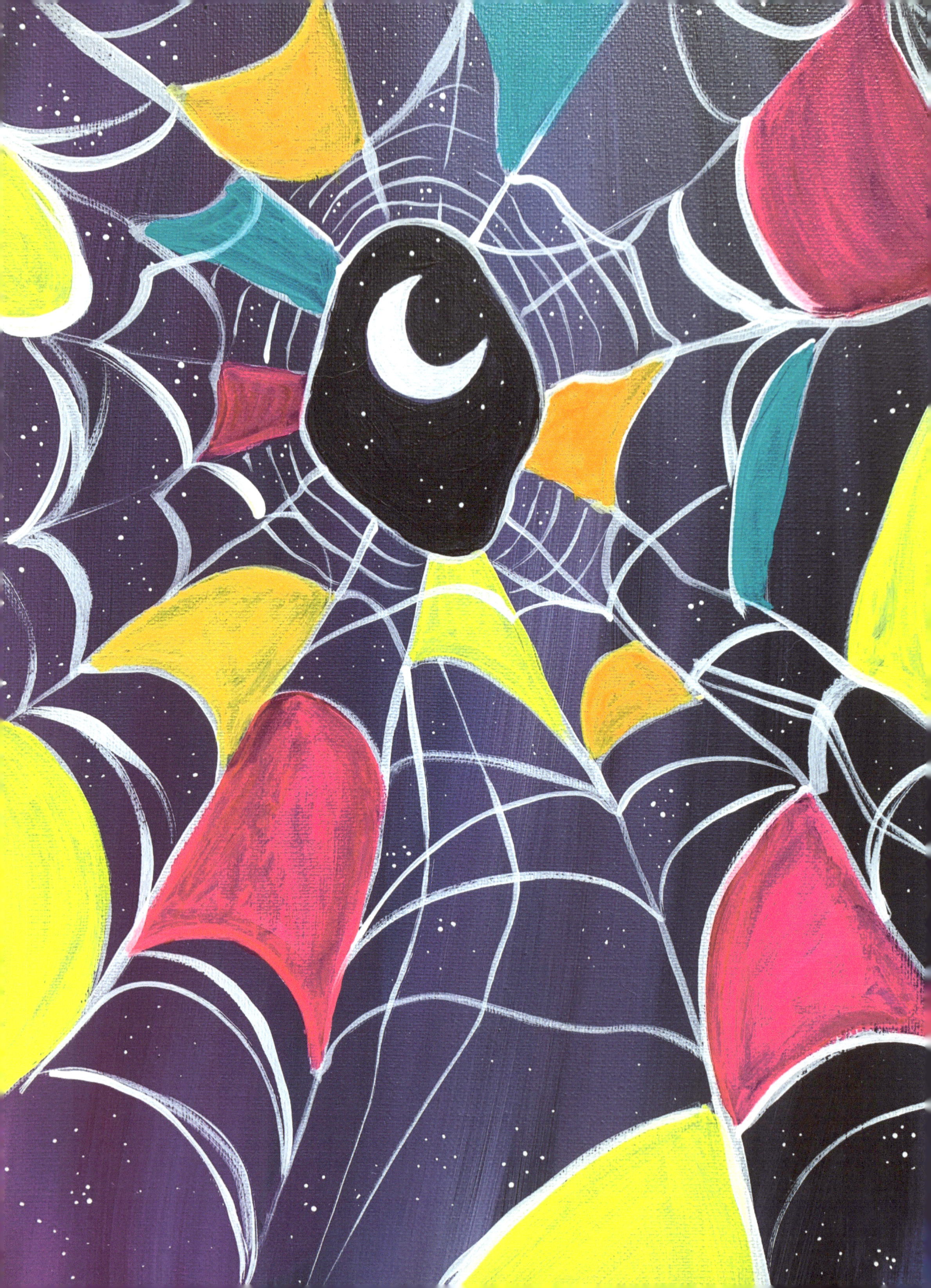

Magic

☾

Wisdom, creativity, and balance of the spider
Through delicate moonlit webs
Bringing light into the darkness
She embodies the light, the dark, and
The magic between creating possibilities and connections
Across the universe

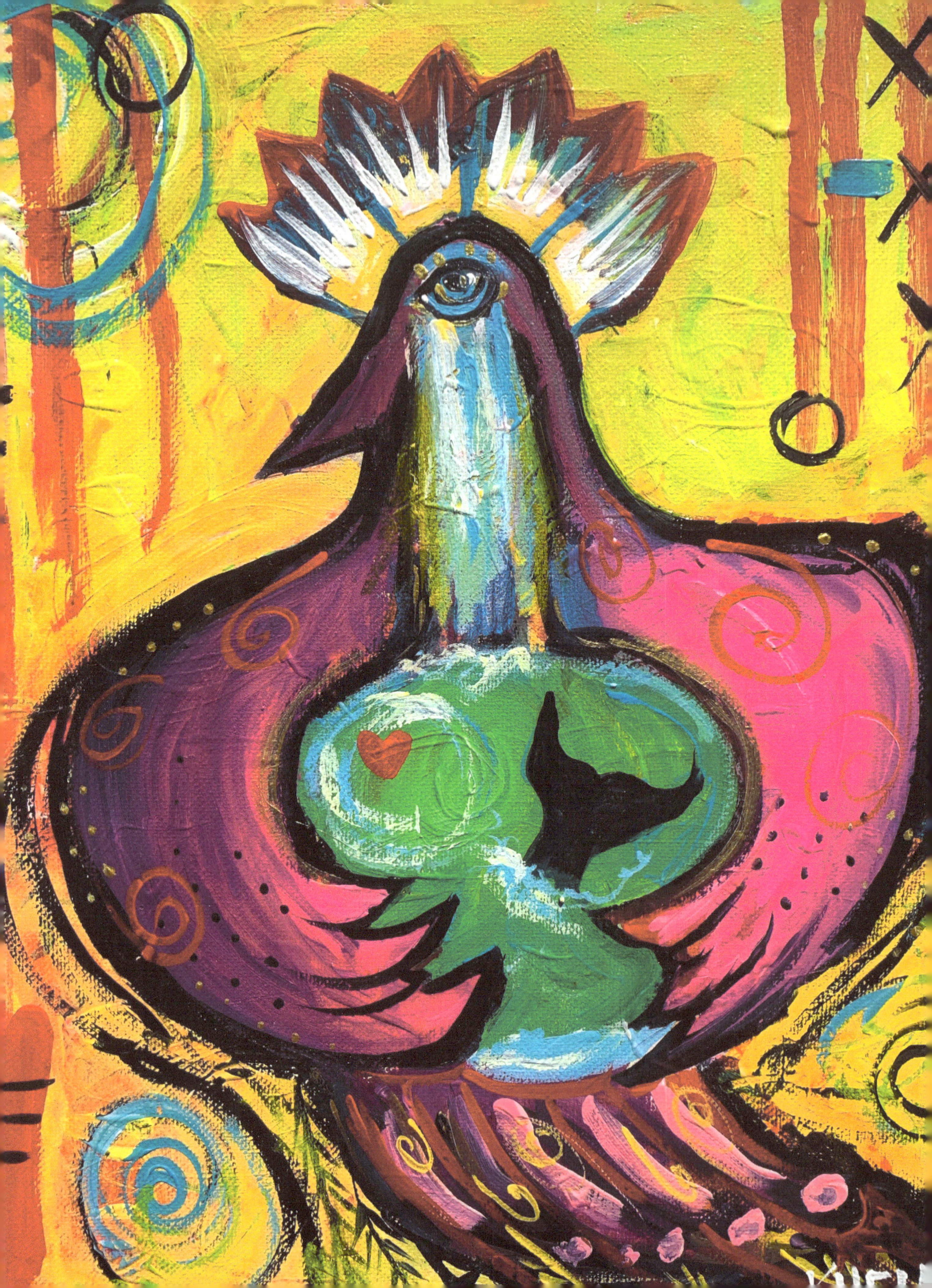

Prayer

Hear the whales call

An ancient language

In a vast sea of majestic creatures

Beneath the horizon

Dive deep into the soul of the past

Tides of healing and change

Turbulent and calm

Washing over the stuck energies of the earth

Inviting renewal in each break of a wave

Water within us,

Water connects us

Be still

Breathe in

Let the tides roll over you

Breathe out

Breathe in

Let the tides renew you

Breathe out

Breathe in

Let the tides heal you

Breathe out

Thank you mother ocean for your strength

Thank you for your ability to purge, cleanse, and heal

Thank you for your resilience

In gratitude each and every day

Let this be your prayer.

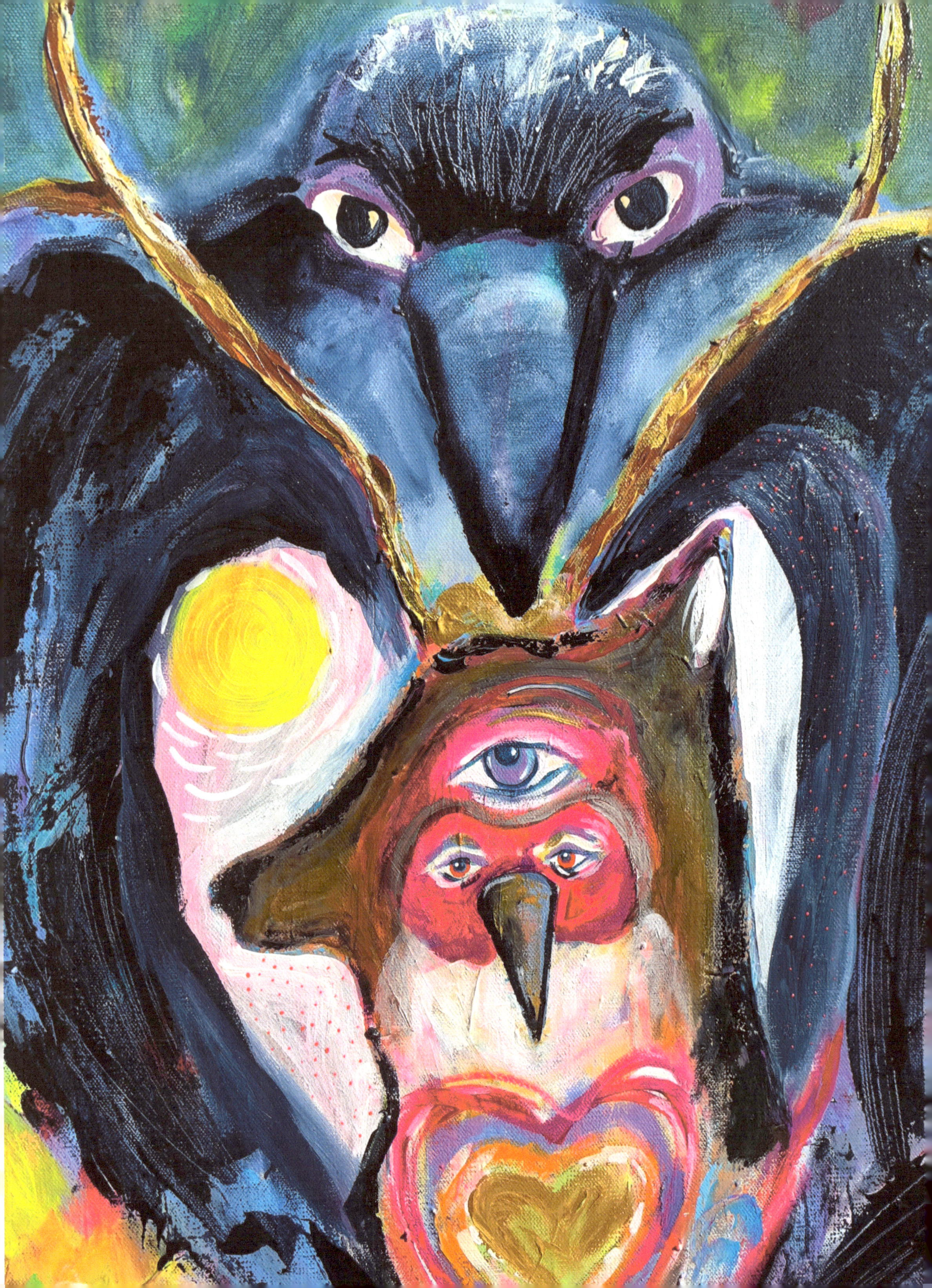

Self

I am the crow

Full of magic and alchemy

I am the deer

Fluid and gentle

I am the owl

Seeing the shadow and honoring wisdom

I am the snake

Healing layer by layer

Creative energies are my divine rights

Fire (of earth)

Transformation (of being)

Growth (of soul)

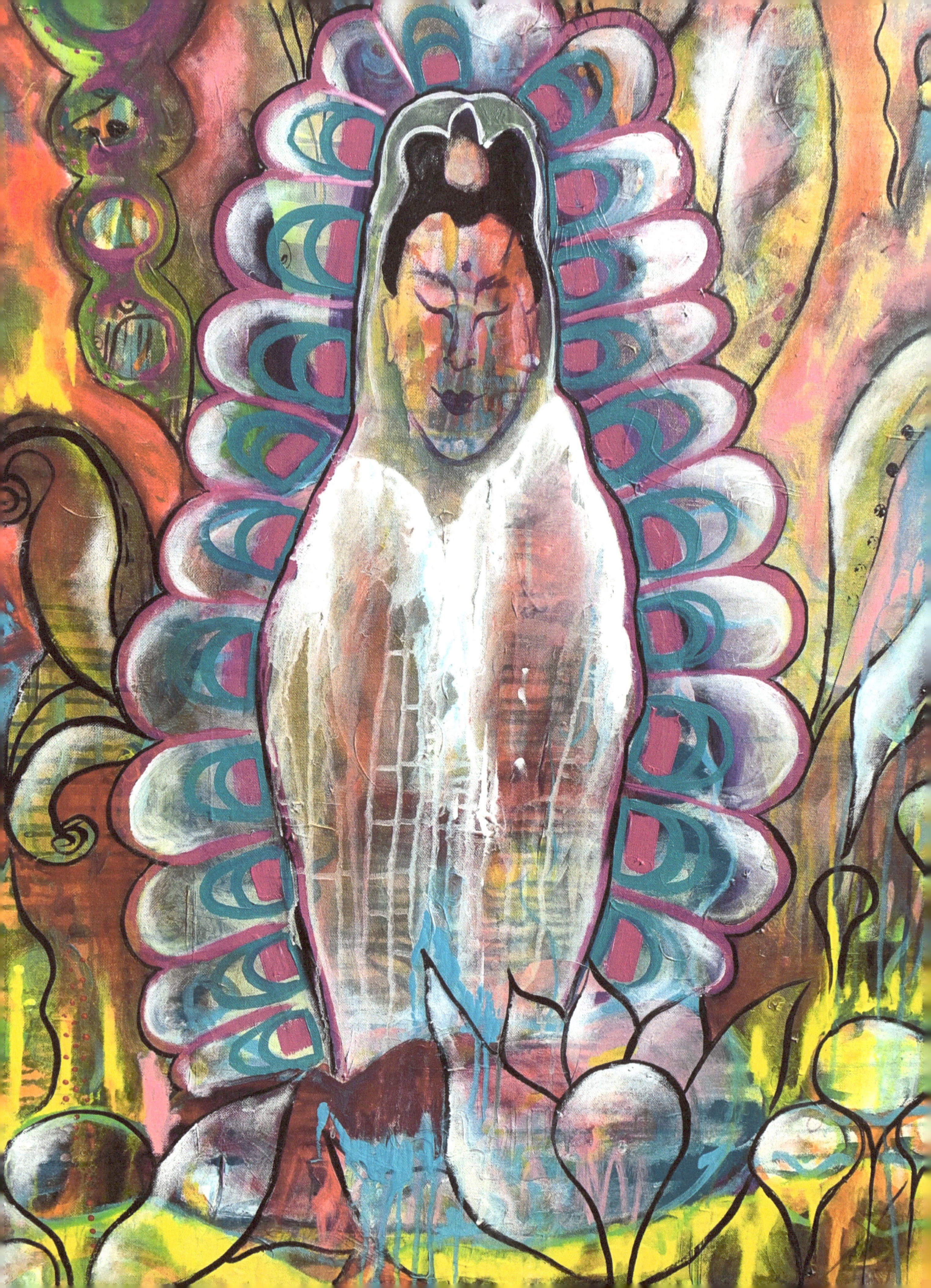

Compassion

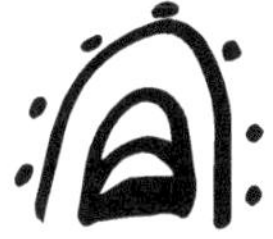

Kwan Yin
Mother Mary
Lady of Guadalupe
Women of compassion
With open hearts

Forgiveness
Listening
Embracing our flaws
Healing with wisdom and grace

For sisters all over the world
We are all connected
We stand together
We embrace challenges
We claim our truths
We find strength in being

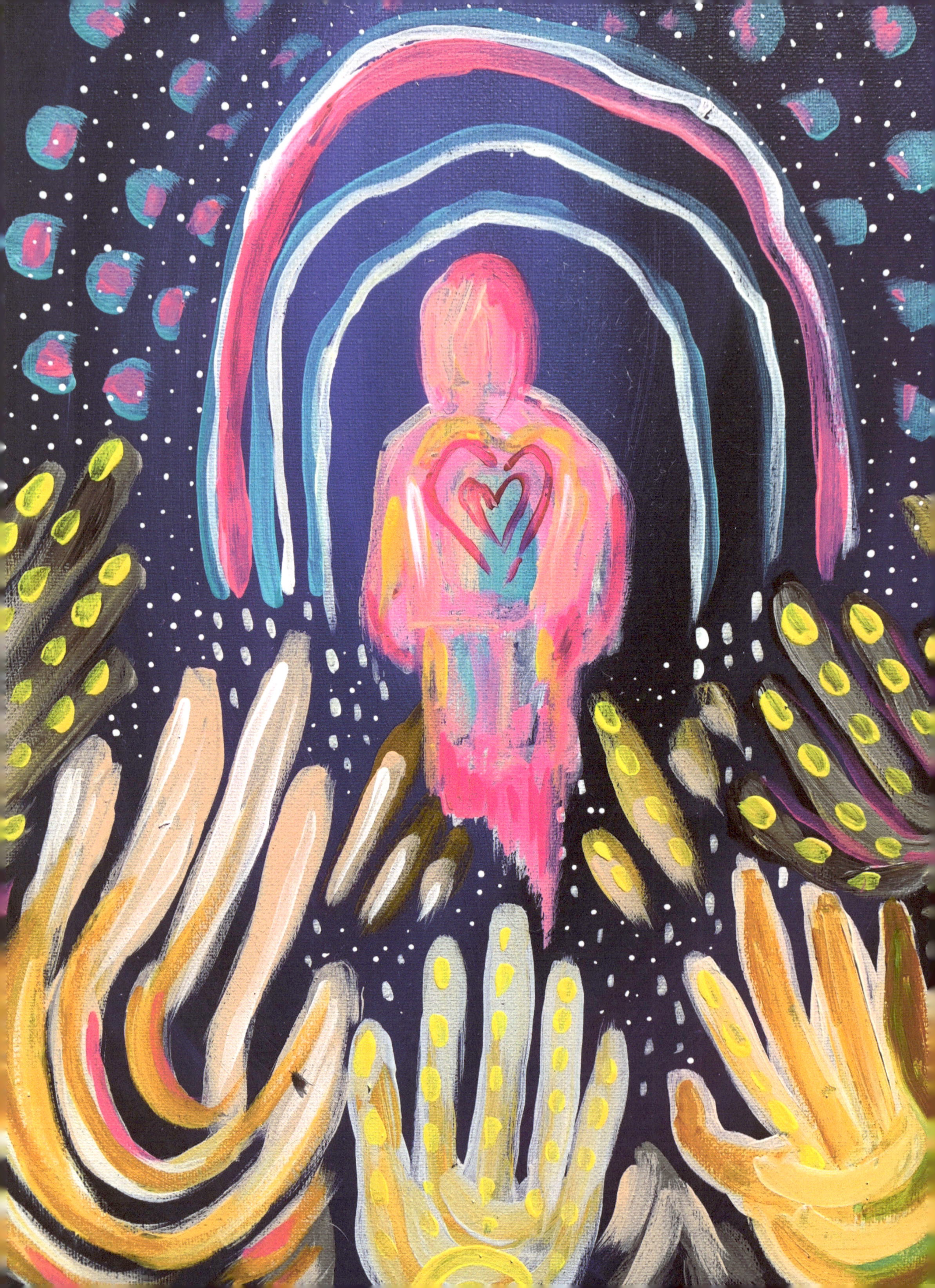

Community

Honest connections

Open communication

Support of a thousand hands

The recognition that you are not alone

Makes the days seem brighter

The heart dance,

And the soul expand

Knowing

You are seen

You are heard

You are held

In a deep resonance of love, respect, community

This community calls the heart

... Home

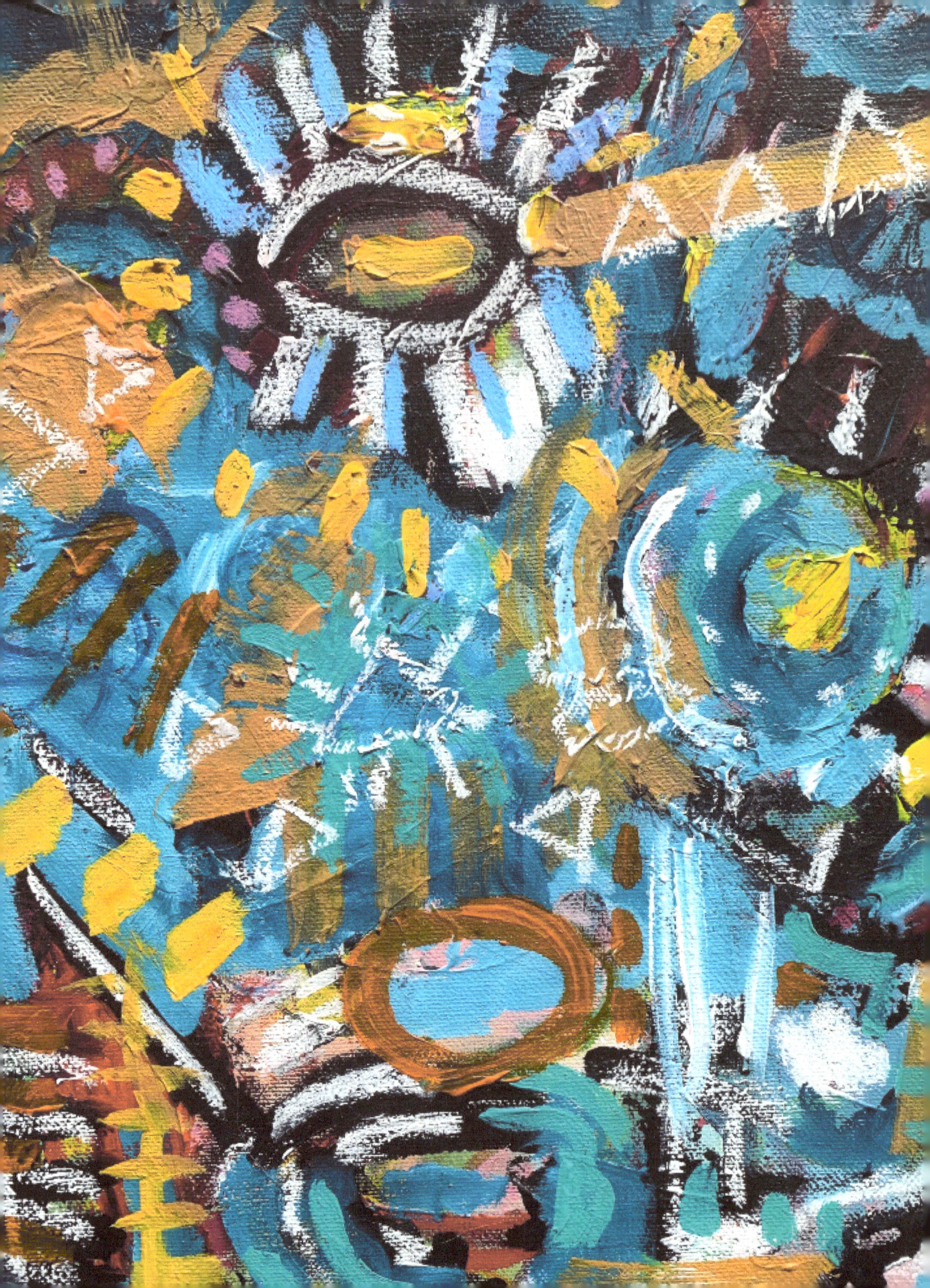

Shadow

Dreams, awareness, advice, and stories
Run through our blood and bones
Breath and desire
Sight and sound
It is our calling to recognize the gifts within these
The deepest parts of ourselves act as a personal radar
For truth and growth
The question is ....
Are
  You
    Willing
      To
        Explore ?

The choice is yours
Though I can say with certainty
The richness lies in the places that are
Uncomfortable
and perhaps scary
Sometimes in the shadows of ourselves
Sometimes in the light of others
And if we are brave enough or even a little
And we face it, question it, understand it and grow
A gift is given
And for that we re-pattern our DNA, our lineage
We become the ancestors
And our stories become the songs generations sing about

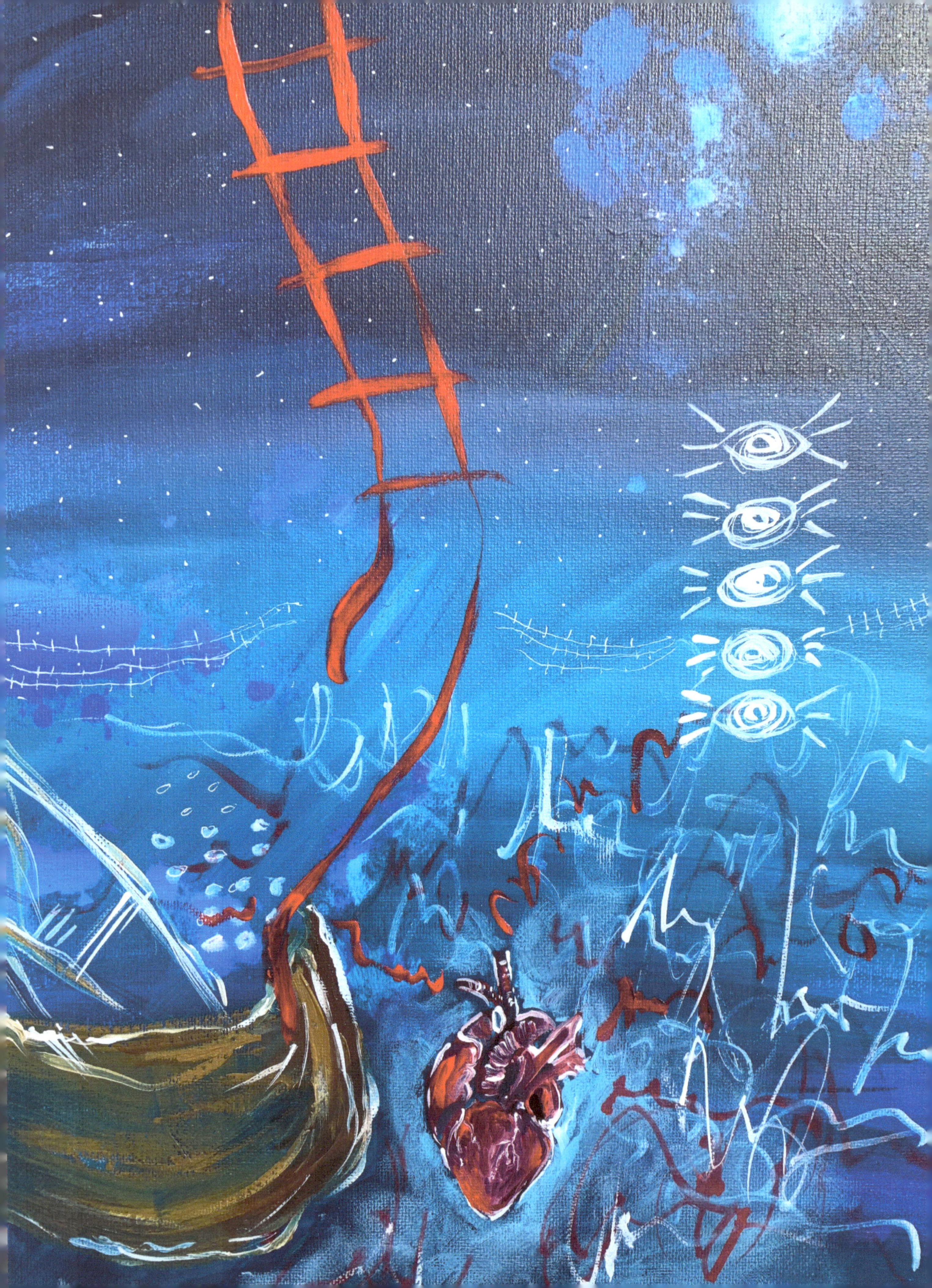

Retrieval

A constant invitation of exploration and risk

To unearth soil and roots

Fertilize, churn

Sowing the seeds that connect to the heart

Offering guidance and respite to the soul

Engaging in a rhythmic ebb and flow

Cycles that surround us

As we dive deeper and deeper

Within the murky water to uncover

The lost ship swallowed by the sea

Finding its heart

And with gratitude and respect

Returning it to the surface

About me

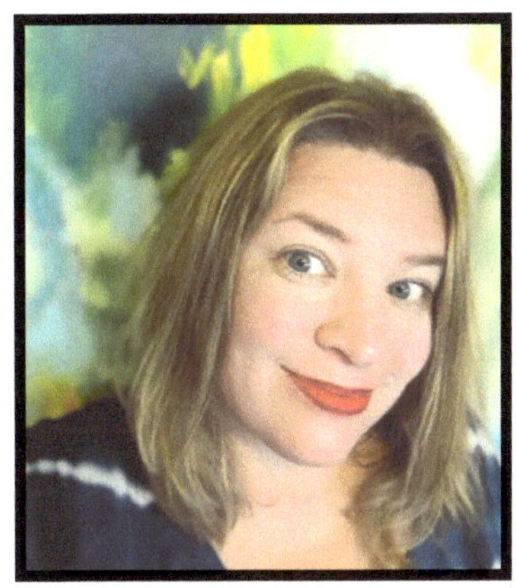

I am an intuitive artist, creative explorer, seeker of awe, nature lover, believer in magic, and wisdom keeper. Art has always been an important and constant guide in my life.

As a warrior for sacred expression and a space holder for deep personal work, I guide individuals to find healing through rediscovering their creativity and authentic voice through the art process. I believe art has the ability to provide insights, to resolve internal conflicts, and most importantly to heal. To me, creating art is a sacred act, as it allows one to recreate the deepest parts of themselves over and over again as they grow, change, and evolve. The good, the bad, and the messy are all embraced. The process of creating art becomes the journey to igniting your sacred truths.

As you engage in the art and words in this book, I invite you to embrace your own magnificent uniqueness, just as you are, right here, right now. Dive deep into curiosity, truth, and the wisdom of your own divine intuition.

With gratitude,

Kimberly

More books by Kimberly Heil

***Gifts of Spirit: Animals and their natural gifts**

2016 Purple Dragonfly Award Winner

***Gifts of Spirit: Animals and their natural gifts**

2018 Purple Dragonfly 1st Place Award Winner

Open up the lines of communication with your child. From Gerry Giraffe's gifts of reaching for the stars, to Otis the Owl's gifts of deep listening, you and your child will be able to discuss and explore your own unique gifts and talents through the animals. Both 32-page books are filled with bold colors and fun animals to delight children of all ages. Snuggle up and get closer as a family as you explore each animal through Gifts of Spirit.

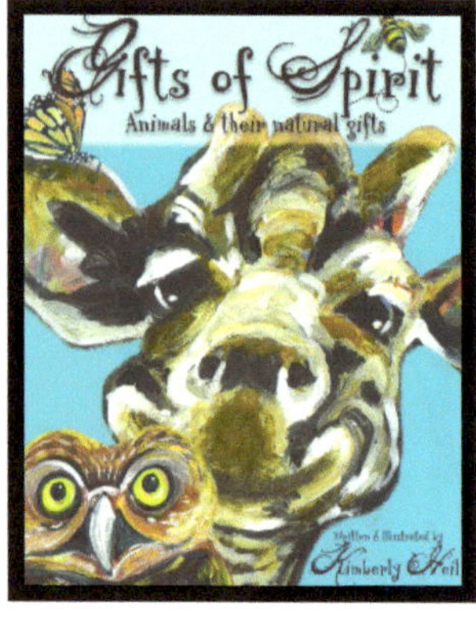

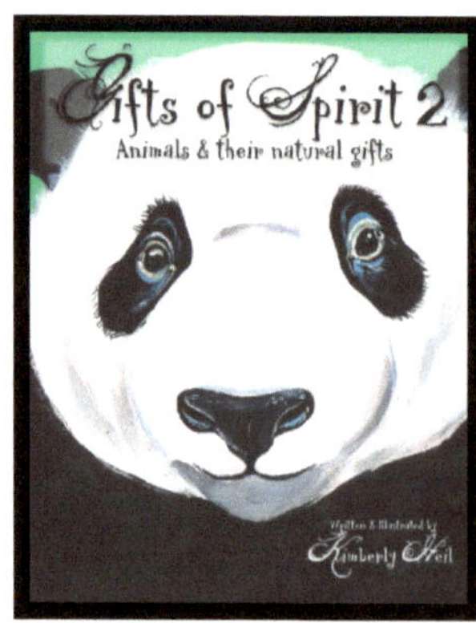

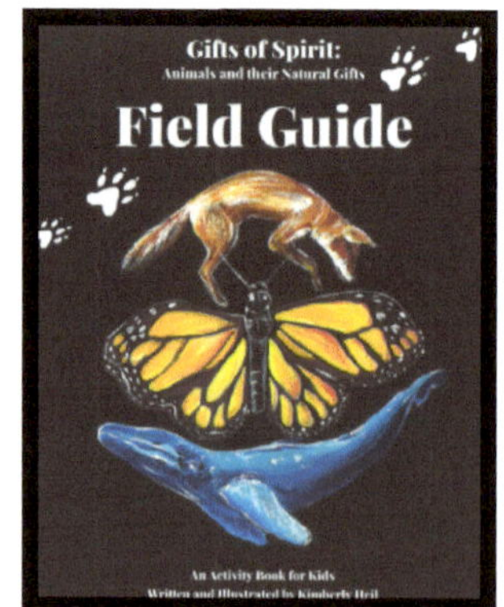

***Gifts of Spirit: Animals and their natural gifts**

Field Guide

A hands-on field guide for kids of all ages. A fun and creative way for kids to connect with nature by observing and documenting their own experiences of the amazing world of animals that surround us daily. Each entry a child makes invites exploration, curiosity, mindfulness, compassion, and sparks creative thinking.

***Gifts of Spirit Animal Card Deck**

This beautifully inspired deck is an invitation to deepen the exploration of the animals and their natural gifts while continuing to encourage kids of all ages to discover and embrace their own unique gifts that they bring to the world. As a valuable resource, this deck offers the opportunity to inspire deeper conversations regarding personal values, strengths, active listening, and problem solving, while helping to cultivate deeper insights and personal confidence, as well as spark creative thinking.

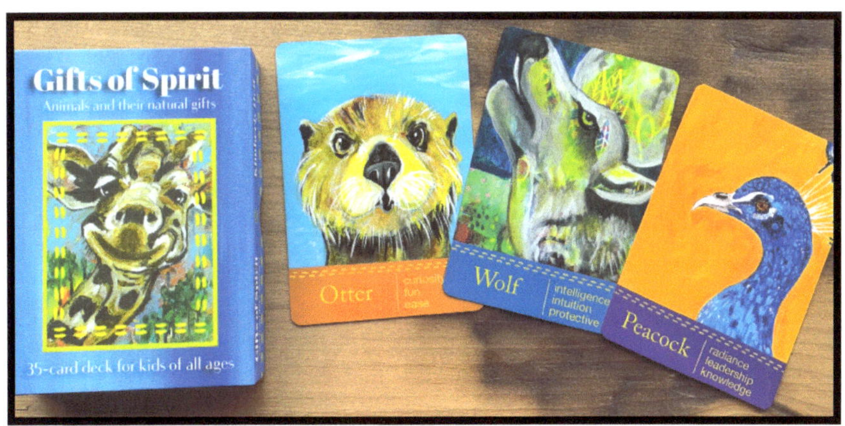

www.ingramcontent.com/pod-product-compliance
Lightning Source LLC
LaVergne TN
LVHW070154110826
845147LV00002B/400
* 9 7 8 0 9 9 9 6 6 3 2 3 3 *